TRANZLATY

Language is for everyone

اللغة للجميع

Beauty and the Beast

الجمال والوحش

Gabrielle-Suzanne Barbot de Villeneuve

English / العربية

Copyright © 2025 Tranzlaty
All rights reserved
Published by Tranzlaty
ISBN: 978-1-83566-965-5
Original text by Gabrielle-Suzanne Barbot de Villeneuve
La Belle et la Bête
First published in French in 1740
Taken from The Blue Fairy Book (Andrew Lang)
Illustration by Walter Crane
www.tranzlaty.com

There was once a rich merchant
كان هناك ذات يوم تاجر ثري
this rich merchant had six children
كان لهذا التاجر الغني ستة أطفال
he had three sons and three daughters
كان لديه ثلاثة أبناء وثلاث بنات
he spared no cost for their education
لم يدخر أي جهد في سبيل تعليمهم
because he was a man of sense
لأنه كان رجلاً عاقلاً
but he gave his children many servants
ولكنه أعطى أولاده العديد من الخدم
his daughters were extremely pretty
كانت بناته جميلات للغاية
and his youngest daughter was especially pretty
وكانت ابنته الصغرى جميلة بشكل خاص
as a child her Beauty was already admired
عندما كانت طفلة كان جمالها محل إعجاب بالفعل
and the people called her by her Beauty
وكان الناس يسمونها بجمالها
her Beauty did not fade as she got older
لم يذبل جمالها مع تقدمها في السن
so the people kept calling her by her Beauty
فكان الناس ينادونها بجمالها
this made her sisters very jealous
وهذا جعل أخواتها يشعرن بالغيرة الشديدة
the two eldest daughters had a great deal of pride
كانت ابنتي الأكبر سناً تتمتعان بقدر كبير من الفخر
their wealth was the source of their pride
ثروتهم كانت مصدر فخرهم
and they didn't hide their pride either
ولم يخفوا كبريائهم أيضًا
they did not visit other merchants' daughters
ولم يزوروا بنات التجار الآخرين
because they only meet with aristocracy
لأنهم لا يلتقون إلا بالأرستقراطية

they went out every day to parties
كانوا يخرجون كل يوم إلى الحفلات
balls, plays, concerts, and so forth
الكرات والمسرحيات والحفلات الموسيقية وما إلى ذلك
and they laughed at their youngest sister
وضحكوا على أختهم الصغرى
because she spent most of her time reading
لأنها قضت معظم وقتها في القراءة
it was well known that they were wealthy
وكان معروفا أنهم أثرياء
so several eminent merchants asked for their hand
لذلك تقدم العديد من التجار البارزين بطلباتهم
but they said they were not going to marry
لكنهم قالوا أنهم لن يتزوجوا
but they were prepared to make some exceptions
لكنهم كانوا مستعدين لعمل بعض الاستثناءات
"perhaps I could marry a Duke"
"ربما أستطيع الزواج من دوق"
"I guess I could marry an Earl"
"أعتقد أنني أستطيع الزواج من إيرل"
Beauty very civilly thanked those that proposed to her
شكرت الجميلة بكل أدب أولئك الذين تقدموا لها
she told them she was still too young to marry
قالت لهم أنها مازالت صغيرة على الزواج
she wanted to stay a few more years with her father
أرادت البقاء مع والدها لبضع سنوات أخرى
All at once the merchant lost his fortune
فجأة خسر التاجر ثروته
he lost everything apart from a small country house
لقد فقد كل شيء باستثناء منزل ريفي صغير
and he told his children with tears in his eyes:
وقال لأولاده والدموع في عينيه :
"we must go to the countryside"
"يجب علينا أن نذهب إلى الريف "
"and we must work for our living"
"ويجب علينا أن نعمل من أجل معيشتنا "

the two eldest daughters didn't want to leave the town
لم ترغب الابنتان الأكبران في مغادرة المدينة

they had several lovers in the city
كان لديهم العديد من العشاق في المدينة

and they were sure one of their lovers would marry them
وكانوا متأكدين من أن أحد عشاقهم سيتزوجهم

they thought their lovers would marry them even with no fortune
ظنوا أن عشاقهم سيتزوجون منهم حتى لو لم يكن لديهم ثروة

but the good ladies were mistaken
لكن السيدات الطيبات أخطأن

their lovers abandoned them very quickly
أحبائهم تخلى عنهم بسرعة كبيرة

because they had no fortunes any more
لأنهم لم يعد لديهم ثروات

this showed they were not actually well liked
أظهر هذا أنهم لم يكونوا محبوبين في الواقع

everybody said they do not deserve to be pitied
قال الجميع أنهم لا يستحقون الشفقة

"we are glad to see their pride humbled"
"نحن سعداء برؤية كبريائهم متواضعًا"

"let them be proud of milking cows"
"فليفتخروا بحلب الأبقار"

but they were concerned for Beauty
لكنهم كانوا مهتمين بالجمال

she was such a sweet creature
لقد كانت مخلوقة لطيفة للغاية

she spoke so kindly to poor people
لقد تحدثت بلطف شديد مع الفقراء

and she was of such an innocent nature
وكانت ذات طبيعة بريئة

Several gentlemen would have married her
كان من الممكن أن يتزوجها العديد من السادة

they would have married her even though she was poor
كانوا ليتزوجوها حتى لو كانت فقيرة

but she told them she couldn't marry them

لكنها أخبرتهم أنها لا تستطيع الزواج منهم

because she would not leave her father

لأنها لن تترك والدها

she was determined to go with him to the countryside

كانت عازمة على الذهاب معه إلى الريف

so that she could comfort and help him

حتى تتمكن من مواساته ومساعدته

Poor Beauty was very grieved at first

لقد حزنت الجميلة المسكينة كثيرًا في البداية

she was grieved by the loss of her fortune

لقد حزنت على فقدان ثروتها

"but crying won't change my fortunes"

"ولكن البكاء لن يغير من حظي"

"I must try to make myself happy without wealth"

"يجب أن أحاول أن أجعل نفسي سعيدًا بدون ثروة"

they came to their country house

لقد جاءوا إلى منزلهم الريفي

and the merchant and his three sons applied themselves to husbandry

والتاجر وأبناؤه الثلاثة اشتغلوا بالزراعة

Beauty rose at four in the morning

وردة الجمال في الرابعة صباحا

and she hurried to clean the house

وسارعت لتنظيف البيت

and she made sure dinner was ready

وتأكدت من أن العشاء جاهز

in the beginning she found her new life very difficult

في البداية وجدت حياتها الجديدة صعبة للغاية

because she had not been used to such work

لأنها لم تكن معتادة على مثل هذا العمل

but in less than two months she grew stronger

لكن في أقل من شهرين أصبحت أقوى

and she was healthier than ever before

وكانت أكثر صحة من أي وقت مضى

after she had done her work she read

بعد أن انتهت من عملها قرأت

she played on the harpsichord

لقد لعبت على القيثارة

or she sung whilst she spun silk

أو غنت وهي تغزل الحرير

on the contrary, her two sisters did not know how to spend their time

على العكس من ذلك، لم تعرف شقيقتاها كيف تقضيان وقتهما

they got up at ten and did nothing but laze about all day

استيقظوا في الساعة العاشرة ولم يفعلوا شيئًا سوى الاسترخاء طوال اليوم

they lamented the loss of their fine clothes

لقد حزنوا على فقدان ملابسهم الجميلة

and they complained about losing their acquaintances

واشتكوا من فقدان معارفهم

"Have a look at our youngest sister," they said to each other

"انظروا إلى أختنا الصغرى "قالوا لبعضهم البعض

"what a poor and stupid creature she is"

"يا لها من مخلوقة فقيرة وغبية "

"it is mean to be content with so little"

"من السيء أن ترضى بالقليل "

the kind merchant was of quite a different opinion

كان للتاجر اللطيف رأي مختلف تمامًا

he knew very well that Beauty outshone her sisters

كان يعلم جيدًا أن الجمال يتفوق على أخواتها

she outshone them in character as well as mind

لقد تفوقت عليهم في الشخصية والعقل

he admired her humility and her hard work

لقد أعجب بتواضعها وعملها الجاد

but most of all he admired her patience

لكن أكثر ما أعجبه هو صبرها

her sisters left her all the work to do

تركت لها أخواتها كل العمل لتقوم به

and they insulted her every moment

وأهانوها في كل لحظة

The family had lived like this for about a year

عاشت العائلة على هذا النحو لمدة عام تقريبًا

then the merchant got a letter from an accountant

ثم حصل التاجر على رسالة من المحاسب
he had an investment in a ship
كان لديه استثمار في سفينة
and the ship had safely arrived
وقد وصلت السفينة بسلامة
this news turned the heads of the two eldest daughters
لقد حرك هذا الخبر رؤوس ابنتيهما الأكبر سنا
they immediately had hopes of returning to town
كان لديهم على الفور أمل في العودة إلى المدينة
because they were quite weary of country life
لأنهم كانوا متعبين جدًا من الحياة الريفية
they went to their father as he was leaving
ذهبوا إلى أبيهم وهو يغادر
they begged him to buy them new clothes
توسلوا إليه أن يشتري لهم ملابس جديدة
dresses, ribbons, and all sorts of little things
الفساتين والشرائط وجميع أنواع الأشياء الصغيرة
but Beauty asked for nothing
لكن الجمال لم يطلب شيئا
because she thought the money wasn't going to be enough
لأنها اعتقدت أن المال لن يكون كافيا
there wouldn't be enough to buy everything her sisters wanted
لن يكون هناك ما يكفي لشراء كل ما تريده أخواتها
"What would you like, Beauty?" asked her father
"ماذا تريدين يا جميلة؟ "سأل والدها
"thank you, father, for the goodness to think of me," she said
"شكرًا لك يا أبي على حسن تفكيرك بي"، قالت
"father, be so kind as to bring me a rose"
"أبي، كن لطيفًا واحضر لي وردة "
"because no roses grow here in the garden"
"لأن الورود لا تنمو هنا في الحديقة "
"and roses are a kind of rarity"
"والورود نوع من الندرة "
Beauty didn't really care for roses
الجمال لم يهتم بالورود حقًا

she only asked for something not to condemn her sisters
لقد طلبت فقط شيئًا لا تدين به أخواتها
but her sisters thought she asked for roses for other reasons
لكن أخواتها اعتقدن أنها طلبت الورود لأسباب أخرى
"she did it just to look particular"
"لقد فعلت ذلك فقط لتبدو مميزة"
The kind man went on his journey
ذهب الرجل الطيب في رحلته
but when he arrived they argued about the merchandise
ولكن عندما وصل تجادلوا حول البضاعة
and after a lot of trouble he came back as poor as before
وبعد الكثير من المتاعب عاد فقيرًا كما كان من قبل
he was within a couple of hours of his own house
كان على بعد بضع ساعات من منزله
and he already imagined the joy of seeing his children
وقد تخيل بالفعل فرحة رؤية أطفاله
but when going through forest he got lost
ولكن عندما مر عبر الغابة فقد ضل طريقه
it rained and snowed terribly
لقد هطلت الأمطار والثلوج بشدة
the wind was so strong it threw him off his horse
كانت الرياح قوية لدرجة أنها ألقته من فوق حصانه
and night was coming quickly
وكان الليل قادمًا بسرعة
he began to think that he might starve
بدأ يفكر أنه قد يموت جوعاً
and he thought that he might freeze to death
وظن أنه قد يتجمد حتى الموت
and he thought wolves may eat him
وظن أن الذئاب قد تأكله
the wolves that he heard howling all round him
الذئاب التي سمعها تعوي من حوله
but all of a sudden he saw a light
ولكن فجأة رأى ضوءًا
he saw the light at a distance through the trees
لقد رأى الضوء من مسافة بعيدة من خلال الأشجار

when he got closer he saw the light was a palace
عندما اقترب رأى أن الضوء كان قصرًا

the palace was illuminated from top to bottom
تم إضاءة القصر من الأعلى إلى الأسفل

the merchant thanked God for his luck
شكر التاجر الله على حظه

and he hurried to the palace
وأسرع إلى القصر

but he was surprised to see no people in the palace
ولكنه فوجئ بعدم وجود أي شخص في القصر

the court yard was completely empty
كانت ساحة المحكمة فارغة تماما

and there was no sign of life anywhere
ولم يكن هناك أي علامة على الحياة في أي مكان

his horse followed him into the palace
وتبعه حصانه إلى القصر

and then his horse found large stable
ثم وجد حصانه اسطبلًا كبيرًا

the poor animal was almost famished
كان الحيوان المسكين جائعا تقريبا

so his horse went in to find hay and oats
فذهب حصانه للبحث عن التبن والشوفان

fortunately he found plenty to eat
لحسن الحظ أنه وجد الكثير ليأكله

and the merchant tied his horse up to the manger
وربط التاجر حصانه في المذود

walking towards the house he saw no one
كان يمشي نحو المنزل ولم ير أحدا

but in a large hall he found a good fire
ولكن في قاعة كبيرة وجد نار جيدة

and he found a table set for one
ووجد مائدة معدة لشخص واحد

he was wet from the rain and snow
كان مبللاً من المطر والثلج

so he went near the fire to dry himself
فذهب إلى النار ليجفف نفسه

"I hope the master of the house will excuse me"
"أتمنى أن يعذرني صاحب البيت"
"I suppose it won't take long for someone to appear"
"أعتقد أنه لن يستغرق الأمر وقتًا طويلاً حتى يظهر شخص ما"
He waited a considerable time
لقد انتظر وقتا طويلا
he waited until it struck eleven, and still nobody came
انتظر حتى دقت الساعة الحادية عشرة، ولم يأت أحد.
at last he was so hungry that he could wait no longer
في النهاية كان جائعًا جدًا لدرجة أنه لم يعد قادرًا على الانتظار
he took some chicken and ate it in two mouthfuls
أخذ بعض الدجاج وأكله في لقمتين
he was trembling while eating the food
كان يرتجف أثناء تناول الطعام
after this he drank a few glasses of wine
وبعد ذلك شرب بضعة أكواب من النبيذ
growing more courageous he went out of the hall
أصبح أكثر شجاعة وخرج من القاعة
and he crossed through several grand halls
وعبر عبر العديد من القاعات الكبرى
he walked through the palace until he came into a chamber
سار في القصر حتى وصل إلى غرفة
a chamber which had an exceeding good bed in it
غرفة بها سرير جيد للغاية
he was very much fatigued from his ordeal
لقد كان مرهقًا جدًا من محنته
and the time was already past midnight
وكان الوقت قد تجاوز منتصف الليل بالفعل
so he decided it was best to shut the door
لذلك قرر أنه من الأفضل إغلاق الباب
and he concluded he should go to bed
وقرر أنه يجب أن يذهب إلى السرير
It was ten in the morning when the merchant woke up
كانت الساعة العاشرة صباحًا عندما استيقظ التاجر
just as he was going to rise he saw something
عندما كان على وشك النهوض رأى شيئًا

he was astonished to see a clean set of clothes
لقد اندهش عندما رأى مجموعة من الملابس النظيفة
in the place where he had left his dirty clothes
في المكان الذي ترك فيه ملابسه المتسخة
"certainly this palace belongs to some kind fairy"
"من المؤكد أن هذا القصر ينتمي إلى نوع من الجنيات"
"a fairy who has seen and pitied me"
"جنية رأتني وأشفقت علي"
he looked through a window
لقد نظر من خلال النافذة
but instead of snow he saw the most delightful garden
ولكن بدلاً من الثلج رأى الحديقة الأكثر روعة
and in the garden were the most beautiful roses
وفي الحديقة كانت أجمل الورود
he then returned to the great hall
ثم عاد إلى القاعة الكبرى
the hall where he had had soup the night before
القاعة التي تناول فيها الحساء في الليلة السابقة
and he found some chocolate on a little table
ووجد بعض الشوكولاتة على طاولة صغيرة
"Thank you, good Madam Fairy," he said aloud
"شكرًا لك، سيدتي الجنية الطيبة"، قال بصوت عالٍ
"thank you for being so caring"
"شكرا لك على اهتمامك الكبير"
"I am extremely obliged to you for all your favours"
"أنا ممتن جدًا لك على كل خدماتك"
the kind man drank his chocolate
الرجل الطيب شرب الشوكولاتة
and then he went to look for his horse
ثم ذهب للبحث عن حصانه
but in the garden he remembered Beauty's request
ولكن في الحديقة تذكر طلب الجمال
and he cut off a branch of roses
وقطع غصن الورد
immediately he heard a great noise
فسمع على الفور ضجة عظيمة

and he saw a terribly frightful Beast
ورأى وحشًا مخيفًا للغاية

he was so scared that he was ready to faint
لقد كان خائفا للغاية لدرجة أنه كان على وشك الإغماء

"You are very ungrateful," said the Beast to him
"أنت جاحد جدًا" قال له الوحش

and the Beast spoke in a terrible voice
وتكلم الوحش بصوت رهيب

"I have saved your life by allowing you into my castle"
"لقد أنقذت حياتك بالسماح لك بالدخول إلى قلعتي"

"and for this you steal my roses in return?"
"و لهذا تسرق الورود مني في المقابل؟"

"The roses which I value beyond anything"
"الورود التي أقدرها أكثر من أي شيء"

"but you shall die for what you've done"
"ولكنك سوف تموت بسبب ما فعلته"

"I give you but a quarter of an hour to prepare yourself"
"أعطيك ربع ساعة فقط لتحضير نفسك"

"get yourself ready for death and say your prayers"
"جهز نفسك للموت وقل صلواتك"

the merchant fell on his knees
سقط التاجر على ركبتيه

and he lifted up both his hands
ورفع كلتا يديه

"My lord, I beseech you to forgive me"
"سيدي أرجوك أن تسامحني"

"I had no intention of offending you"
"لم يكن لدي أي نية لإهانتك"

"I gathered a rose for one of my daughters"
"جمعت وردة لإحدى بناتي"

"she asked me to bring her a rose"
"طلبت مني أن أحضر لها وردة"

"I am not your lord, but I am a Beast," replied the monster
"أنا لست سيدك، بل أنا وحش"، أجاب الوحش.

"I don't love compliments"
"أنا لا أحب المجاملات"

"I like people who speak as they think"
"أنا أحب الأشخاص الذين يتحدثون كما يفكرون "

"do not imagine I can be moved by flattery"
"لا أتصور أنني يمكن أن أتأثر بالمجاملة "

"But you say you have got daughters"
"ولكنك تقول أن لديك بنات "

"I will forgive you on one condition"
"سأسامحك بشرط واحد "

"one of your daughters must come to my palace willingly"
"يجب على إحدى بناتك أن تأتي إلى قصري طوعًا "

"and she must suffer for you"
"ولابد أن تعاني من أجلك "

"Let me have your word"
"دعني أحصل على كلمتك "

"and then you can go about your business"
"وبعد ذلك يمكنك أن تذهب إلى عملك "

"Promise me this:"
"وعدني بهذا":

"if your daughter refuses to die for you, you must return within three months"
"إذا رفضت ابنتك أن تموت من أجلك، فيجب عليك العودة خلال ثلاثة أشهر "

the merchant had no intentions to sacrifice his daughters
لم يكن لدى التاجر أي نية للتضحية ببناته

but, since he was given time, he wanted to see his daughters once more
لكن بما أنه حصل على الوقت، أراد أن يرى بناته مرة أخرى

so he promised he would return
فوعد بأنه سيعود

and the Beast told him he might set out when he pleased
فقال له الوحش أنه يستطيع الانطلاق عندما يشاء

and the Beast told him one more thing
وقال له الوحش شيئا آخر

"you shall not depart empty handed"
"لن تغادر خالي الوفاض "

"go back to the room where you lay"

"ارجع إلى الغرفة التي ترقد فيها "
"you will see a great empty treasure chest"
"سوف ترى صندوق كنز كبير فارغ "
"fill the treasure chest with whatever you like best"
"املأ صندوق الكنز بما تفضله "
"and I will send the treasure chest to your home"
"وسأرسل صندوق الكنز إلى منزلك "
and at the same time the Beast withdrew
وفي نفس الوقت انسحب الوحش
"Well," said the good man to himself
حسنًا، "قال الرجل الصالح لنفسه
"if I must die, I shall at least leave something to my children"
"إذا كان لا بد لي من الموت، فسوف أترك شيئًا لأطفالي على الأقل "
so he returned to the bedchamber
فعاد إلى حجرة النوم
and he found a great many pieces of gold
ووجد قطعًا كثيرة من الذهب
he filled the treasure chest the Beast had mentioned
ملأ صندوق الكنز الذي ذكره الوحش
and he took his horse out of the stable
وأخرج حصانه من الإسطبل
the joy he felt when entering the palace was now equal to the grief he felt leaving it
لقد كانت الفرحة التي شعر بها عند دخول القصر تعادل الحزن الذي شعر به عند مغادرته .
the horse took one of the roads of the forest
أخذ الحصان أحد طرق الغابة
and in a few hours the good man was home
وفي غضون ساعات قليلة كان الرجل الصالح في منزله
his children came to him
جاء إليه أولاده
but instead of receiving their embraces with pleasure, he looked at them
ولكن بدلاً من أن يستقبلهم بكل سرور، نظر إليهم
he held up the branch he had in his hands

رفع الفرع الذي كان بين يديه

and then he burst into tears

ثم انفجر بالبكاء

"Beauty," he said, "please take these roses"

"يا جميلة، "قال،" من فضلك خذي هذه الورود "

"you can't know how costly these roses have been"

"لا يمكنك أن تعرف كم كانت تكلفة هذه الورود "

"these roses have cost your father his life"

"هذه الورود كلفت والدك حياته "

and then he told of his fatal adventure

ثم تحدث عن مغامرته المميتة

immediately the two eldest sisters cried out

على الفور صرخت الأختان الأكبر سنا

and they said many mean things to their beautiful sister

وقالوا الكثير من الأشياء السيئة لأختهم الجميلة

but Beauty did not cry at all

ولكن الجمال لم يبكي على الإطلاق

"Look at the pride of that little wretch," said they

"انظروا إلى كبرياء هذا الوغد الصغير "قالوا

"she did not ask for fine clothes"

"لم تطلب ملابس جميلة "

"she should have done what we did"

"كان ينبغي لها أن تفعل ما فعلناه "

"she wanted to distinguish herself"

"أرادت أن تميز نفسها "

"so now she will be the death of our father"

"لذلك الآن سوف تكون موت والدنا "

"and yet she does not shed a tear"

"ومع ذلك فهي لا تذرف دمعة "

"Why should I cry?" answered Beauty

"لماذا أبكي؟ "أجابت الجميلة

"crying would be very needless"

"البكاء سيكون بلا داعٍ "

"my father will not suffer for me"

"لن يعاني والدي من أجلي "

"the monster will accept of one of his daughters"

"الوحش سوف يقبل بواحدة من بناته"

"I will offer myself up to all his fury"

"سأقدم نفسي لكل غضبه"

"I am very happy, because my death will save my father's life"

"أنا سعيد جدًا لأن موتي سينقذ حياة والدي"

"my death will be a proof of my love"

"موتي سيكون دليلا على حبي"

"No, sister," said her three brothers

"لا يا أختي" قال إخوتها الثلاثة

"that shall not be"

"هذا لن يكون"

"we will go find the monster"

"سنذهب للبحث عن الوحش"

"and either we will kill him..."

"وإما أن نقتله..."

"... or we will perish in the attempt"

"...أو سنهلك في المحاولة"

"Do not imagine any such thing, my sons," said the merchant

"لا تتخيلوا مثل هذا الأمر يا أبنائي" قال التاجر

"the Beast's power is so great that I have no hope you could overcome him"

"قوة الوحش عظيمة لدرجة أنني لا أملك أي أمل في أن تتمكن من التغلب عليه"

"I am charmed with Beauty's kind and generous offer"

"أنا مفتون بالعرض الجميل والكريم"

"but I cannot accept to her generosity"

"لكنني لا أستطيع أن أقبل كرمها"

"I am old, and I don't have long to live"

"أنا عجوز، وليس لدي وقت طويل للعيش"

"so I can only loose a few years"

"لذا لا أستطيع أن أخسر سوى بضع سنوات"

"time which I regret for you, my dear children"

"الوقت الذي أندم عليه من أجلكم يا أبنائي الأعزاء"

"But father," said Beauty

"ولكن يا أبي" قال الجمال

"you shall not go to the palace without me"
"لن تذهب إلى القصر بدوني "
"you cannot stop me from following you"
"لا يمكنك منعي من متابعتك "
nothing could convince Beauty otherwise
لا شيء يمكن أن يقنع الجمال بخلاف ذلك
she insisted on going to the fine palace
أصرت على الذهاب إلى القصر الجميل
and her sisters were delighted at her insistence
وفرح أخواتها بإصرارها
The merchant was worried at the thought of losing his daughter
كان التاجر قلقًا من فكرة فقدان ابنته
he was so worried that he had forgotten about the chest full of gold
لقد كان قلقًا للغاية لدرجة أنه نسي الصندوق المليء بالذهب
at night he retired to rest, and he shut his chamber door
وفي الليل ذهب للراحة وأغلق باب غرفته
then, to his great astonishment, he found the treasure by his bedside
ثم، إلى دهشته الكبيرة، وجد الكنز بجانب سريره
he was determined not to tell his children
لقد كان مصمما على عدم إخبار أطفاله
if they knew, they would have wanted to return to town
لو علموا لأرادوا العودة إلى المدينة
and he was resolved not to leave the countryside
وكان عازما على عدم مغادرة الريف
but he trusted Beauty with the secret
لكنه وثق بالجمال في السر
she informed him that two gentlemen had came
فأخبرته أن رجلين قد جاءا
and they made proposals to her sisters
وقدموا لها عروض الزواج من أخواتها
she begged her father to consent to their marriage
توسلت إلى والدها أن يوافق على زواجهما
and she asked him to give them some of his fortune

وطلبت منه أن يعطيهم بعضًا من ثروته
she had already forgiven them
لقد سامحتهم بالفعل
the wicked creatures rubbed their eyes with onions
فركت المخلوقات الشريرة عيونها بالبصل
to force some tears when they parted with their sister
لإجبارهم على البكاء عندما انفصلوا عن أختهم
but her brothers really were concerned
لكن إخوتها كانوا قلقين حقًا
Beauty was the only one who did not shed any tears
كان الجمال هو الوحيد الذي لم يذرف أي دموع
she did not want to increase their uneasiness
لم تكن تريد أن تزيد من قلقهم
the horse took the direct road to the palace
اتخذ الحصان الطريق المباشر إلى القصر
and towards evening they saw the illuminated palace
وفي المساء رأوا القصر المضاء
the horse took himself into the stable again
عاد الحصان إلى الإسطبل مرة أخرى
and the good man and his daughter went into the great hall
ودخل الرجل الصالح وابنته إلى القاعة الكبرى
here they found a table splendidly served up
هنا وجدوا طاولة تم تقديمها بشكل رائع
the merchant had no appetite to eat
لم يكن لدى التاجر شهية للأكل
but Beauty endeavoured to appear cheerful
لكن الجمال سعى إلى الظهور بمظهر مبهج
she sat down at the table and helped her father
جلست على الطاولة وساعدت والدها
but she also thought to herself:
لكنها فكرت في نفسها أيضًا :
"Beast surely wants to fatten me before he eats me"
"إن الوحش يريد بالتأكيد أن يسمنني قبل أن يأكلني "
"that is why he provides such plentiful entertainment"
"لهذا السبب فهو يقدم مثل هذا القدر الوفير من الترفيه "
after they had eaten they heard a great noise

وبعد أن أكلوا سمعوا ضجيجا عظيما

and the merchant bid his unfortunate child farewell, with tears in his eyes

ويودع التاجر ابنه البائس والدموع في عينيه

because he knew the Beast was coming

لأنه كان يعلم أن الوحش قادم

Beauty was terrified at his horrid form

لقد كان الجمال مرعوبًا من شكله البشع

but she took courage as well as she could

لكنها استجمعت شجاعتها قدر استطاعتها

and the monster asked her if she came willingly

وسألها الوحش هل جاءت طوعا

"yes, I have come willingly," she said trembling

"نعم لقد أتيت طوعا "قالت وهي ترتجف

the Beast responded, "You are very good"

فأجابه الوحش" أنت جيد جدًا "

"and I am greatly obliged to you; honest man"

"وأنا ممتن لك كثيرًا أيها الرجل الصادق "

"go your ways tomorrow morning"

"اذهب في طريقك غدًا صباحًا "

"but never think of coming here again"

"ولكن لا تفكر في المجيء إلى هنا مرة أخرى "

"Farewell Beauty, farewell Beast," he answered

"وداعًا أيها الجمال، وداعًا أيها الوحش"، أجاب

and immediately the monster withdrew

وعلى الفور انسحب الوحش

"Oh, daughter," said the merchant

"يا ابنتي "قال التاجر

and he embraced his daughter once more

وعانق ابنته مرة أخرى

"I am almost frightened to death"

"أنا خائفة حتى الموت تقريبًا "

"believe me, you had better go back"

صدقني، من الأفضل أن تعود

"let me stay here, instead of you"

"دعني أبقى هنا، بدلاً منك "

"No, father," said Beauty, in a resolute tone
"لا يا أبي "قالت الجميلة بنبرة حازمة

"you shall set out tomorrow morning"
"سوف تنطلق غدًا صباحًا "

"leave me to the care and protection of providence"
"اتركني لرعاية وحماية العناية الإلهية "

nonetheless they went to bed
ومع ذلك ذهبوا إلى السرير

they thought they would not close their eyes all night
ظنوا أنهم لن يغلقوا أعينهم طوال الليل

but just as they lay down they slept
ولكن عندما استلقوا ناموا

Beauty dreamed a fine lady came and said to her:
حلمت الجميلة أن سيدة جميلة جاءت وقالت لها :

"I am content, Beauty, with your good will"
"أنا راضٍ يا جميلتي عن حسن إرادتك "

"this good action of yours shall not go unrewarded"
"إن هذا العمل الصالح لن يذهب سدى "

Beauty waked and told her father her dream
استيقظت الجميلة وأخبرت والدها بحلمها

the dream helped to comfort him a little
لقد ساعده الحلم على التعزية قليلاً

but he could not help crying bitterly as he was leaving
ولكنه لم يستطع أن يمنع نفسه من البكاء بمرارة وهو يغادر

as soon as he was gone, Beauty sat down in the great hall and cried too
بمجرد رحيله، جلست الجميلة في القاعة الكبرى وبكت أيضًا

but she resolved not to be uneasy
لكنها قررت ألا تشعر بالقلق

she decided to be strong for the little time she had left to live
قررت أن تكون قوية في الوقت القليل المتبقي لها من الحياة

because she firmly believed the Beast would eat her
لأنها كانت تعتقد اعتقادا راسخا أن الوحش سوف يأكلها

however, she thought she might as well explore the palace
ومع ذلك، فقد اعتقدت أنها قد تستكشف القصر أيضًا

and she wanted to view the fine castle

وأرادت أن ترى القلعة الجميلة
a castle which she could not help admiring

قلعة لم تستطع إلا الإعجاب بها
it was a delightfully pleasant palace

لقد كان قصرًا جميلًا وممتعًا
and she was extremely surprised at seeing a door

وكانت مندهشة للغاية عندما رأت الباب
and over the door was written that it was her room

وكان مكتوبا على الباب أنها غرفتها
she opened the door hastily

فتحت الباب بسرعة
and she was quite dazzled with the magnificence of the room

وكانت مبهورة تمامًا بروعة الغرفة
what chiefly took up her attention was a large library

ما لفت انتباهها بشكل رئيسي هو مكتبة كبيرة
a harpsichord and several music books

قيثارة والعديد من الكتب الموسيقية
"Well," said she to herself

"حسنًا" قالت لنفسها
"I see the Beast will not let my time hang heavy"

"أرى أن الوحش لن يترك وقتي معلقًا بثقله"
then she reflected to herself about her situation

ثم فكرت في نفسها بشأن وضعها
"If I was meant to stay a day all this would not be here"

"لو كان من المفترض أن أبقى يومًا واحدًا فلن يكون كل هذا هنا"
this consideration inspired her with fresh courage

ألهمها هذا الاعتبار بشجاعة جديدة
and she took a book from her new library

وأخذت كتابًا من مكتبتها الجديدة
and she read these words in golden letters:

وقرأت هذه الكلمات بأحرف من ذهب :
"Welcome Beauty, banish fear"

"مرحبا بالجمال، نفي الخوف"
"You are queen and mistress here"

"أنت الملكة والسيده هنا"

"Speak your wishes, speak your will"
"تحدث عن رغباتك، تحدث عن إرادتك "
"Swift obedience meets your wishes here"
"الطاعة السريعة تلبي رغباتك هنا "
"Alas," said she, with a sigh
"آه، "قالت وهي تتنهد
"Most of all I wish to see my poor father"
"أكثر ما أتمنى أن أرى والدي المسكين "
"and I would like to know what he is doing"
"وأريد أن أعرف مذا يفعل "
As soon as she had said this she noticed the mirror
بمجرد أن قالت هذا لاحظت المرآة
to her great amazement she saw her own home in the mirror
لقد كانت دهشتها عظيمة عندما رأت منزلها في المرآة
her father arrived emotionally exhausted
وصل والدها منهكًا عاطفيًا
her sisters went to meet him
ذهبت أخواتها لمقابلته
despite their attempts to appear sorrowful, their joy was visible
على الرغم من محاولاتهم للظهور بمظهر الحزين، إلا أن فرحتهم كانت واضحة .
a moment later everything disappeared
وبعد لحظة اختفى كل شيء
and Beauty's apprehensions disappeared too
واختفت مخاوف الجمال أيضًا
for she knew she could trust the Beast
لأنها كانت تعلم أنها تستطيع أن تثق بالوحش
At noon she found dinner ready
وفي الظهيرة وجدت العشاء جاهزا
she sat herself down at the table
جلست على الطاولة
and she was entertained with a concert of music
واستمتعت بحفل موسيقي
although she couldn't see anybody
على الرغم من أنها لم تستطع رؤية أي شخص

at night she sat down for supper again
وفي الليل جلست لتتناول العشاء مرة أخرى
this time she heard the noise the Beast made
هذه المرة سمعت صوت الوحش
and she could not help being terrified
ولم تستطع أن تمنع نفسها من الخوف
"Beauty," said the monster
"الجمال "قال الوحش
"do you allow me to eat with you?"
هل تسمح لي بتناول الطعام معك؟
"do as you please," Beauty answered trembling
"افعل ما يحلو لك "أجابت الجميلة وهي ترتجف
"No," replied the Beast
"لا "أجاب الوحش
"you alone are mistress here"
" أنت وحدك السيدة هنا"
"you can send me away if I'm troublesome"
" يمكنك أن ترسلني بعيدًا إذا كنت مزعجًا"
"send me away and I will immediately withdraw"
" أرسلني بعيدًا وسوف أنسحب على الفور"
"But, tell me; do you not think I am very ugly?"
" ولكن أخبرني، هل لا تعتقد أنني قبيح جدًا؟"
"That is true," said Beauty
"هذا صحيح "قالت الجميلة
"I cannot tell a lie"
" لا أستطيع أن أقول كذبة"
"but I believe you are very good natured"
" لكنني أعتقد أنك طيب القلب جدًا"
"I am indeed," said the monster
"أنا كذلك بالفعل "قال الوحش
"But apart from my ugliness, I also have no sense"
" ولكن بصرف النظر عن قبحى، ليس لدي أي إحساس أيضًا"
"I know very well that I am a silly creature"
" أنا أعلم جيدًا أنني مخلوق سخيف"
"It is no sign of folly to think so," replied Beauty
"ليس من الحماقة أن نفكر بهذه الطريقة "أجابت الجميلة

"Eat then, Beauty," said the monster
"كل إذن يا جميلتي "قال الوحش

"try to amuse yourself in your palace"
"حاول أن تسلي نفسك في قصرك "

"everything here is yours"
"كل شيء هنا لك "

"and I would be very uneasy if you were not happy"
"وسأكون قلقًا جدًا إذا لم تكن سعيدًا "

"You are very obliging," answered Beauty
"أنت متعاون للغاية "أجابت الجميلة

"I admit I am pleased with your kindness"
"أعترف أنني مسرور بلطفك "

"and when I consider your kindness, I hardly notice your deformities"
"وعندما أفكر في لطفك، بالكاد ألاحظ تشوهاتك "

"Yes, yes," said the Beast, "my heart is good
"نعم، نعم، "قال الوحش،" قلبي طيب

"but although I am good, I am still a monster"
"لكن على الرغم من أنني جيد، إلا أنني لا أزال وحشًا "

"There are many men that deserve that name more than you"
"هناك العديد من الرجال الذين يستحقون هذا الاسم أكثر منك "

"and I prefer you just as you are"
"وأنا أفضلك كما أنت "

"and I prefer you more than those who hide an ungrateful heart"
"وأنا أفضلك على الذين يخفون قلبا لا يشكرون "

"if only I had some sense," replied the Beast
"لو كان لدي بعض العقل "أجاب الوحش

"if I had sense I would make a fine compliment to thank you"
"لو كان لدي عقل لأقدم لك مجاملة رائعة لأشكرك "

"but I am so dull"
"لكنني ممل جدًا "

"I can only say I am greatly obliged to you"
"لا أستطيع إلا أن أقول إنني ممتن لك كثيرًا "

Beauty ate a hearty supper

تناولت الجميلة عشاءً شهيًا

and she had almost conquered her dread of the monster

وكانت قد تغلبت تقريبًا على خوفها من الوحش

but she wanted to faint when the Beast asked her the next question

لكنها أرادت أن تغمى عليها عندما سألها الوحش السؤال التالي

"Beauty, will you be my wife?"

"جميلتي هل تقبلين أن تكوني زوجتي؟ "

she took some time before she could answer

استغرق الأمر بعض الوقت قبل أن تتمكن من الإجابة

because she was afraid of making him angry

لأنها كانت خائفة من إغضابها

at last, however, she said "no, Beast"

وفي النهاية قالت" لا يا وحش "

immediately the poor monster hissed very frightfully

على الفور أطلق الوحش المسكين هسهسة مخيفة للغاية

and the whole palace echoed

والقصر كله يردد

but Beauty soon recovered from her fright

لكن الجمال سرعان ما تعافت من خوفها

because Beast spoke again in a mournful voice

لأن الوحش تحدث مرة أخرى بصوت حزين

"then farewell, Beauty"

"ثم وداعا يا جمال "

and he only turned back now and then

ولم يرجع إلا من حين لآخر

to look at her as he went out

لينظر إليها وهو يخرج

now Beauty was alone again

الآن أصبح الجمال وحيدا مرة أخرى

she felt a great deal of compassion

لقد شعرت بقدر كبير من التعاطف

"Alas, it is a thousand pities"

"يا للأسف، إنه لأمر مؤسف "

"anything so good natured should not be so ugly"

"أي شيء طيب القلب لا ينبغي أن يكون قبيحًا جدًا "

Beauty spent three months very contentedly in the palace
قضت الجميلة ثلاثة أشهر سعيدة جدًا في القصر
every evening the Beast paid her a visit
كل مساء كان الوحش يزورها
and they talked during supper
وتحدثوا أثناء العشاء
they talked with common sense
لقد تحدثوا بالفطرة السليمة
but they didn't talk with what people call wittiness
لكنهم لم يتحدثوا بما يسميه الناس بالذكاء
Beauty always discovered some valuable character in the Beast
الجمال يكتشف دائمًا بعض السمات القيمة في الوحش
and she had gotten used to his deformity
وقد اعتادت على تشوهه
she didn't dread the time of his visit anymore
لم تعد تخشى موعد زيارته
now she often looked at her watch
الآن كانت تنظر إلى ساعتها كثيرًا
and she couldn't wait for it to be nine o'clock
ولم تستطع الانتظار حتى تصبح الساعة التاسعة
because the Beast never missed coming at that hour
لأن الوحش لم يتأخر عن المجيء في تلك الساعة
there was only one thing that concerned Beauty
لم يكن هناك سوى شيء واحد يتعلق بالجمال
every night before she went to bed the Beast asked her the same question
كل ليلة قبل أن تذهب إلى السرير كان الوحش يسألها نفس السؤال
the monster asked her if she would be his wife
سألها الوحش هل ستكون زوجته
one day she said to him, "Beast, you make me very uneasy"
ذات يوم قالت له" أيها الوحش، أنت تجعلني أشعر بالقلق الشديد "
"I wish I could consent to marry you"
"أتمنى أن أتمكن من الموافقة على الزواج منك "
"but I am too sincere to make you believe I would marry you"

- 25 -

"لكنني صادقة جدًا بحيث لا أستطيع أن أجعلك تصدق أنني سأتزوجك "
"our marriage will never happen"
"زواجنا لن يتم أبدًا "
"I shall always see you as a friend"
"سوف أراك دائمًا كصديق "
"please try to be satisfied with this"
"من فضلك حاول أن تكون راضيًا بهذا "
"I must be satisfied with this," said the Beast
"يجب أن أكون راضيًا بهذا "قال الوحش
"I know my own misfortune"
"أنا أعرف سوء حظي "
"but I love you with the tenderest affection"
"لكنني أحبك بأحر المشاعر "
"However, I ought to consider myself as happy"
"ومع ذلك، ينبغي لي أن أعتبر نفسي سعيدًا "
"and I should be happy that you will stay here"
"وسأكون سعيدًا لأنك ستبقى هنا "
"promise me never to leave me"
"وعدني أن لا تتركني أبدًا "
Beauty blushed at these words
احمر وجه الجمال عند سماع هذه الكلمات
one day Beauty was looking in her mirror
ذات يوم كانت الجمال تنظر في مرآتها
her father had worried himself sick for her
كان والدها قلقًا عليها للغاية
she longed to see him again more than ever
لقد كانت تتوق لرؤيته مرة أخرى أكثر من أي وقت مضى
"I could promise never to leave you entirely"
"أستطيع أن أعدك بأنني لن أتركك أبدًا "
"but I have so great a desire to see my father"
"لكن لدي رغبة كبيرة في رؤية والدي "
"I would be impossibly upset if you say no"
"سوف أكون مستاءً للغاية إذا قلت لا "
"I had rather die myself," said the monster
"أفضل أن أموت بنفسي "قال الوحش
"I would rather die than make you feel uneasiness"

"أفضل أن أموت بدلاً من أن أجعلك تشعر بالقلق "
"I will send you to your father"
"سأرسلك إلى أبيك "
"you shall remain with him"
"سوف تبقى معه "
"and this unfortunate Beast will die with grief instead"
"وسيموت هذا الوحش التعيس حزنًا بدلًا من ذلك "
"No," said Beauty, weeping
"لا "قالت الجميلة باكية
"I love you too much to be the cause of your death"
"أنا أحبك كثيرًا لدرجة أنني لا أستطيع أن أكون سبب موتك "
"I give you my promise to return in a week"
"أعدك بالعودة خلال أسبوع "
"You have shown me that my sisters are married"
"لقد أظهرت لي أن أخواتي متزوجات "
"and my brothers have gone to the army"
"وأخوتي ذهبوا إلى الجيش "
"let me stay a week with my father, as he is alone"
"دعني أبقى مع والدي لمدة أسبوع، فهو وحيد "
"You shall be there tomorrow morning," said the Beast
"ستكون هناك غدًا في الصباح"، قال الوحش
"but remember your promise"
"ولكن تذكر وعدك "
"You need only lay your ring on a table before you go to bed"
"كل ما عليك فعله هو وضع خاتمك على الطاولة قبل الذهاب إلى السرير "
"and then you will be brought back before the morning"
"ثم ترجعون قبل الصباح "
"Farewell dear Beauty," sighed the Beast
"وداعًا يا عزيزتي أنجميلة "تنهد الوحش
Beauty went to bed very sad that night
ذهبت الجميلة إلى السرير حزينة جدًا تلك الليلة
because she didn't want to see Beast so worried
لأنها لم ترغب في رؤية الوحش قلقًا للغاية
the next morning she found herself at her father's home
وفي صباح اليوم التالي وجدت نفسها في منزل والدها

she rung a little bell by her bedside
لقد قرعت جرسًا صغيرًا بجانب سريرها
and the maid gave a loud shriek
وأطلقت الخادمة صرخة عالية
and her father ran upstairs
وركض والدها إلى الطابق العلوي
he thought he was going to die with joy
كان يعتقد أنه سيموت فرحًا
he held her in his arms for quarter of an hour
لقد احتضنها بين ذراعيه لمدة ربع ساعة
eventually the first greetings were over
في النهاية انتهت التحية الأولى
Beauty began to think of getting out of bed
بدأت الجمال تفكر في الخروج من السرير
but she realized she had brought no clothes
لكنها أدركت أنها لم تحضر أي ملابس
but the maid told her she had found a box
لكن الخادمة قالت لها أنها وجدت صندوقا
the large trunk was full of gowns and dresses
كان الصندوق الكبير مليئا بالفساتين والعباءات
each gown was covered with gold and diamonds
كان كل ثوب مغطى بالذهب والماس
Beauty thanked Beast for his kind care
شكرت الجميلة الوحش على رعايته الطيبة
and she took one of the plainest of the dresses
وأخذت واحدة من أبسط الفساتين
she intended to give the other dresses to her sisters
كانت تنوي إعطاء الفساتين الأخرى لأخواتها
but at that thought the chest of clothes disappeared
ولكن في تلك اللحظة اختفى صندوق الملابس
Beast had insisted the clothes were for her only
أصر الوحش على أن الملابس كانت لها فقط
her father told her that this was the case
أخبرها والدها أن هذا هو الحال
and immediately the trunk of clothes came back again
وعلى الفور عادت خزانة الملابس مرة أخرى

Beauty dressed herself with her new clothes
ارتدت الجميلة ملابسها الجديدة

and in the meantime maids went to find her sisters
وفي هذه الأثناء ذهبت الخادمات للبحث عن أخواتها

both her sister were with their husbands
وكانت أختاها مع زوجيهما

but both her sisters were very unhappy
لكن أختيها كانتا غير سعيدتين للغاية

her eldest sister had married a very handsome gentleman
تزوجت أختها الكبرى من رجل وسيم للغاية

but he was so fond of himself that he neglected his wife
ولكنه كان يحب نفسه كثيرًا لدرجة أنه أهمل زوجته

her second sister had married a witty man
تزوجت أختها الثانية من رجل ذكي

but he used his wittiness to torment people
ولكنه استخدم ذكائه لتعذيب الناس

and he tormented his wife most of all
وكان يعذب زوجته أكثر من أي شيء آخر

Beauty's sisters saw her dressed like a princess
رأت أخوات الجميلة أنها ترتدي ملابس مثل الأميرة

and they were sickened with envy
فأصابهم الحسد

now she was more beautiful than ever
الآن أصبحت أكثر جمالا من أي وقت مضى

her affectionate behaviour could not stifle their jealousy
لم يتمكن سلوكها الحنون من تهدئة غيرتهم

she told them how happy she was with the Beast
قالت لهم كم كانت سعيدة بالوحش

and their jealousy was ready to burst
وكانت غيرتهم على وشك الانفجار

They went down into the garden to cry about their misfortune
نزلوا إلى الحديقة يبكون على مصيبتهم

"In what way is this little creature better than us?"
"بأي طريقة يكون هذا المخلوق الصغير أفضل منا؟ "

"Why should she be so much happier?"

"لماذا يجب أن تكون أكثر سعادة؟"

"Sister," said the older sister

"أختي "قالت الأخت الكبرى

"a thought just struck my mind"

"فكرة خطرت ببالي للتو"

"let us try to keep her here for more than a week"

"دعونا نحاول إبقاءها هنا لأكثر من أسبوع"

"perhaps this will enrage the silly monster"

"ربما هذا سوف يثير غضب الوحش السخيف"

"because she would have broken her word"

"لأنها كانت ستخالف وعدها"

"and then he might devour her"

"وبعد ذلك قد يلتهمها"

"that's a great idea," answered the other sister

"هذه فكرة رائعة "أجابت الأخت الأخرى

"we must show her as much kindness as possible"

"يجب علينا أن نظهر لها أكبر قدر ممكن من اللطف"

the sisters made this their resolution

الأخوات اتخذن هذا القرار

and they behaved very affectionately to their sister

وكانوا يتصرفون مع أختهم بلطف شديد

poor Beauty wept for joy from all their kindness

بكت الجميلة الفقيرة من الفرح بسبب كل لطفهم

when the week was expired, they cried and tore their hair

عندما انتهى الأسبوع، بكوا ومزقوا شعرهم

they seemed so sorry to part with her

لقد بدوا حزينين جدًا لفراقها

and Beauty promised to stay a week longer

ووعد الجمال بالبقاء لمدة أسبوع أطول

In the meantime, Beauty could not help reflecting on herself

في هذه الأثناء، لم تستطع الجمال أن تتوقف عن التفكير في نفسها

she worried what she was doing to poor Beast

كانت قلقة بشأن ما كانت تفعله للوحش المسكين

she know that she sincerely loved him

إنها تعلم أنها أحبته بصدق

and she really longed to see him again

وكانت تتوق حقا لرؤيته مرة أخرى
the tenth night she spent at her father's too
الليلة العاشرة التي قضتها في منزل والدها أيضًا
she dreamed she was in the palace garden
حلمت أنها في حديقة القصر
and she dreamt she saw the Beast extended on the grass
وحلمت أنها رأت الوحش ممتدا على العشب
he seemed to reproach her in a dying voice
بدا وكأنه يوبخها بصوت يحتضر
and he accused her of ingratitude
واتهمها بالجحود
Beauty woke up from her sleep
استيقظت الجميلة من نومها
and she burst into tears
وانفجرت في البكاء
"Am I not very wicked?"
" هل أنا لست شريرة جدًا؟ "
"Was it not cruel of me to act so unkindly to the Beast?"
" ألم يكن من القسوة من جانبي أن أتصرف بمثل هذه القسوة تجاه الوحش؟ "
"Beast did everything to please me"
" الوحش فعل كل شيء لإرضائي "
"Is it his fault that he is so ugly?"
" هل هو خطؤه أنه قبيح جدًا؟ "
"Is it his fault that he has so little wit?"
" هل هو خطؤه أنه لديه القليل من الذكاء؟ "
"He is kind and good, and that is sufficient"
" إنه طيب وطيب وهذا يكفي "
"Why did I refuse to marry him?"
لماذا رفضت الزواج منه؟
"I should be happy with the monster"
" يجب أن أكون سعيدًا بالوحش "
"look at the husbands of my sisters"
" أنظر إلى أزواج أخواتي "
"neither wittiness, nor a being handsome makes them good"
" لا الذكاء ولا المظهر الجيد يجعلهم جيدين "
"neither of their husbands makes them happy"

"لا أحد من أزواجهن يسعدهن "
"but virtue, sweetness of temper, and patience"
"لكن الفضيلة وحسن الخلق والصبر "
"these things make a woman happy"
"هذه الأشياء تجعل المرأة سعيدة "
"and the Beast has all these valuable qualities"
"والوحش لديه كل هذه الصفات القيمة "
"it is true; I do not feel the tenderness of affection for him"
"هذا صحيح؛ فأنا لا أشعر بحنان المودة تجاهه "
"but I find I have the highest gratitude for him"
"لكنني أجد أنني أشعر بالامتنان الشديد له "
"and I have the highest esteem of him"
"وأنا أقدره تقديرا عاليا "
"and he is my best friend"
"وهو أفضل صديق لي "
"I will not make him miserable"
"لن أجعله بائسًا "
"If were I to be so ungrateful I would never forgive myself"
"لو كنت جاحدًا إلى هذا الحد فلن أسامح نفسي أبدًا "
Beauty put her ring on the table
وضعت الجميلة خاتمها على الطاولة
and she went to bed again
وذهبت إلى السرير مرة أخرى
scarce was she in bed before she fell asleep
لم تكن في السرير قبل أن تغفو
she woke up again the next morning
استيقظت مرة أخرى في الصباح التالي
and she was overjoyed to find herself in the Beast's palace
وكانت في غاية السعادة عندما وجدت نفسها في قصر الوحش
she put on one of her nicest dress to please him
ارتدت أحد أجمل فساتينها لإرضائه
and she patiently waited for evening
وانتظرت المساء بصبر
at last the wished-for hour came
جاءت الساعة المرجوة
the clock struck nine, yet no Beast appeared

دقت الساعة التاسعة، ولكن لم يظهر أي وحش

Beauty then feared she had been the cause of his death

ثم خافت الجميلة أن تكون سبب وفاته

she ran crying all around the palace

ركضت وهي تبكي في كل أنحاء القصر

after having sought for him everywhere, she remembered her dream

بعد أن بحثت عنه في كل مكان، تذكرت حلمها

and she ran to the canal in the garden

وركضت إلى القناة في الحديقة

there she found poor Beast stretched out

هناك وجدت الوحش المسكين ممددًا

and she was sure she had killed him

وكانت متأكدة أنها قتلته

she threw herself upon him without any dread

ألقت بنفسها عليه دون أي خوف

his heart was still beating

كان قلبه لا يزال ينبض

she fetched some water from the canal

لقد جلبت بعض الماء من القناة

and she poured the water on his head

وصبّت الماء على رأسه

the Beast opened his eyes and spoke to Beauty

فتح الوحش عينيه وتحدث إلى الجمال

"You forgot your promise"

" لقد نسيت وعدك "

"I was so heartbroken to have lost you"

" لقد كنت حزينًا جدًا لفقدك "

"I resolved to starve myself"

" لقد قررت أن أجوع نفسي "

"but I have the happiness of seeing you once more"

" لكنني أشعر بالسعادة لرؤيتك مرة أخرى "

"so I have the pleasure of dying satisfied"

" لذلك لدي متعة الموت راضيا "

"No, dear Beast," said Beauty, "you must not die"

" لا يا عزيزي الوحش،" قالت الجميلة،" لا يجب أن تموت "

"Live to be my husband"
"أعيش لكي أكون زوجي "
"from this moment I give you my hand"
"من هذه اللحظة أعطيك يدي "
"and I swear to be none but yours"
"وأنا أقسم أن لا أكون إلا لك "
"Alas! I thought I had only a friendship for you"
"آه !كنت أعتقد أن لدي صداقة معك فقط "
"but the grief I now feel convinces me;"
"لكن الحزن الذي أشعر به الآن يقنعني"؛
"I cannot live without you"
"لا أستطيع العيش بدونك "
Beauty scarce had said these words when she saw a light
كانت الجميلة النادره قد قالت هذه الكلمات عندما رأت الضوء
the palace sparkled with light
كان القصر يتلألأ بالضوء
fireworks lit up the sky
الألعاب النارية أضاءت السماء
and the air filled with music
والهواء مملوء بالموسيقى
everything gave notice of some great event
كل شيء أعطى إشعارًا بحدث عظيم
but nothing could hold her attention
ولكن لا شيء يمكن أن يلفت انتباهها
she turned to her dear Beast
التفتت إلى وحشها العزيز
the Beast for whom she trembled with fear
الوحش الذي ارتجفت خوفا منه
but her surprise was great at what she saw!
لكن مفاجأتها كانت عظيمة مما رأته !
the Beast had disappeared
لقد اختفى الوحش
instead she saw the loveliest prince
بدلا من ذلك رأت الأمير الأجمل
she had put an end to the spell
لقد وضعت حدا للتعويذة

a spell under which he resembled a Beast
تعويذة كان يشبه فيها الوحش
this prince was worthy of all her attention
كان هذا الأمير يستحق كل اهتمامها
but she could not help but ask where the Beast was
لكنها لم تستطع إلا أن تسأل أين الوحش؟
"You see him at your feet," said the prince
"أنت تراه عند قدميك "قال الأمير
"A wicked fairy had condemned me"
"لقد أدانتني جنية شريرة "
"I was to remain in that shape until a beautiful princess agreed to marry me"
"لقد كان من المفترض أن أظل على هذا الشكل حتى وافقت أميرة جميلة على الزواج مني "
"the fairy hid my understanding"
"لقد أخفت الجنية فهمي "
"you were the only one generous enough to be charmed by the goodness of my temper"
"لقد كنت الشخص الوحيد الكريم بما يكفي لكي يسحر بطيبة مزاجي "
Beauty was happily surprised
لقد تفاجأت الجمال بسعادة
and she gave the charming prince her hand
وأعطت الأمير الساحر يدها
they went together into the castle
لقد ذهبوا معا إلى القلعة
and Beauty was overjoyed to find her father in the castle
وسعدت الجميلة عندما وجدت والدها في القلعة
and her whole family were there too
وكانت عائلتها بأكملها هناك أيضًا
even the beautiful lady that appeared in her dream was there
حتى السيدة الجميلة التي ظهرت في حلمها كانت هناك
"Beauty," said the lady from the dream
الجمال "قالت السيدة من الحلم
"come and receive your reward"
"تعال واحصل على مكافأتك "
"you have preferred virtue over wit or looks"

"لقد فضّلت الفضيلة على الذكاء أو المظهر "
"and you deserve someone in whom these qualities are united"
"وأنت تستحق شخصًا تتحد فيه هذه الصفات "
"you are going to be a great queen"
"سوف تصبحين ملكة عظيمة "
"I hope the throne will not lessen your virtue"
"أرجو أن لا يقلل العرش من فضيلتك "
then the fairy turned to the two sisters
ثم توجهت الجنية نحو الأختين
"I have seen inside your hearts"
"لقد رأيت داخل قلوبكم "
"and I know all the malice your hearts contain"
"وأنا أعلم كل الحقد الذي في قلوبكم "
"you two will become statues"
"سوف تصبحان تمثالين "
"but you will keep your minds"
"ولكن يجب أن تحافظوا على عقولكم "
"you shall stand at the gates of your sister's palace"
"ستقفين عند أبواب قصر أختك "
"your sister's happiness shall be your punishment"
"سعادة أختك ستكون عقابك "
"you won't be able to return to your former states"
"لن تتمكن من العودة إلى حالتك السابقة "
"unless, you both admit your faults"
"ما لم يعترف كلاكما بأخطائه "
"but I am foresee that you will always remain statues"
"لكنني أتوقع أنكم ستبقون تماثيلًا إلى الأبد "
"pride, anger, gluttony, and idleness are sometimes conquered"
"الكبرياء والغضب والشراهة والكسل يتم التغلب عليها في بعض الأحيان "
"but the conversion of envious and malicious minds are miracles"
"لكن تحويل العقول الحاسدة والخبيثة هو المعجزات "
immediately the fairy gave a stroke with her wand
على الفور قامت الجنية بضربه بعصاها

and in a moment all that were in the hall were transported
وفي لحظة تم نقل كل من كان في القاعة
they had gone into the prince's dominions
لقد ذهبوا إلى ممتلكات الأمير
the prince's subjects received him with joy
واستقبله رعية الأمير بفرح
the priest married Beauty and the Beast
تزوج الكاهن من الجميلة والوحش
and he lived with her many years
وعاش معها سنوات طويلة
and their happiness was complete
وكانت سعادتهم كاملة
because their happiness was founded on virtue
لأن سعادتهم كانت مبنية على الفضيلة

The End
النهاية

www.tranzlaty.com

www.ingramcontent.com/pod-product-compliance
Lightning Source LLC
Chambersburg PA
CBHW012013090526
44590CB00026B/3994